Acknowledgement of Land & of the Traditional Owners of this Land

I would like to acknowledge the Gadigal people of the Eora Nation, upon whose stolen land I stand on today.
I recognise that this land was never terra nullius — the land belonging to these peoples was never ceded, given up, bought or sold.
I would like to pay my respects to Aboriginal Elders past, present and emerging, and I extend this acknowledgement to all Aboriginal and Torres Strait Islander people.

CONTENTS

1: LO♥E Lies Bleeding
(L'AMORE sta Sanguinando)
2: Only Women Bleed
(Solo le Donne Sanguinano)
3: Find What Works for You
(Trova ciò che Funziona per Te)
4: Mind Meld
(Fusione Mentale)
5: Do Not Live in FEAR
(Non Vivere nella PAURA)
6: Apple of Knowledge
(Mela della Conoscenza)
7: The Tree of LO♥E
(L'albero dell'AMORE)
8: Echo Beach
(Spiaggia dell'Eco)
9: Use Me as a "Bad" Example
(Usami Come un Male Esempio)
10: One of "Them"
(Uno di "loro")
11: Steamroller Blues
(Blues Rullo a Vapore)
12: Ignorance is Bliss
(L'ignoranza è Beatitudine)
13: Nothing Else Mattered
(Nient'altro Importava)
14: No More Mr Nice Guy
(Niente Più Signor Bravo Ragazzo)
15: You Are Too Needy
(Sei Troppo Bisognoso)
16: He is the One
(Lui è l'Uno)
17: Do Not Think!
(Non pensare!)

CONTENTS

18: Man Eater
(Mangiatrice di Uomini)
19: Who is Happy Here?
(Chi è Felice Qui?)
20: What's Between Your Legs?
(Cosa c'è tra le tue Gambe?)
21: I'm an Invitor
(Sono un Invitatore)
22: The Midnight Rider
(Il Cavaliere di Mezzanotte)
23: The Challenge
(La Sfida)
24: Unhinged
(Scatenato)
25: Tattooed Woman
(Donna Tatuata)
26: Punk
(Punk)
27: I'm Not Going to Participate
(Non ho Intenzione di Partecipare)
28: Falls in Love with Wealth
(Si Innamora della Ricchezza)
29: I Disagree with Everything You've Said So Far!
(Non sono d'accordo con tutto quello che hai detto finora!)
30: My Demons
(I Miei Demoni)
31: With Age Comes Experience!
(Con l'età Arriva l'Esperienza!)
32: The Head/He♥rt Dichotomy
(La Dicotomia Testa/Cuore)
33: Divine Intervention
(Intervento Divino)
34: Hey, Hey Ho
(Ehi, Ehi Ho)

CONTENTS

35: Where Have They All Gone?
(Dove Sono Finiti Tutti?)
36: Ok!
(Ok!)
37: False Hopes
(False Speranze)
38: The Withdrawal Method
(Il Metodo di Ritiro)
39: I Don't Find You Sexually Attractive
(Non ti Trovo Sessualmente Attraente)
40: I Cannot Piss Straight
(Non Posso Pisciare Dritto)
41: She Uses Sex as Therapy
(Lei Usa il Sesso Come Terapia)
42: My Soil is Fertile
(Il mio Terreno è Fertile)
43: I Exist!
(Io Esisto!)
44: Reboot
(Riavviare)
45: I Am a Player
(Sono un Giocatore)
46: Have a Good LIFE!
(Hanno una Buona vita!)
47: Who Are You Fucking Today?
(Chi Stai Scopando Oggi?)
48: It's Just Life
(È Solo la Vita)
49: Finally, I'm a Hippie
(Finalmente Sono un Hippie)
50: I Don't Need More Information
(Non Ho Bisogno di Ulteriori Informazioni)

LO♥E Lies Bleeding

(L'AMORE sta Sanguinando)

There is blood on my hands.
There is blood on my face.
There is blood on my clothes.
There is blood on the dance floor.
There is blood on the the sheets.
There is blood on the knife that I'm holding in my hands.
There is blood in my HE♥RT.
Because…
…LO♥E lies bleeding.

You stabbed me in my HE♥RT.
You left me bleeding on the floor.
You left me for DEAD.
You just walked out.
You just left.
You never looked back.
And my LO♥E lies bleeding.

"The Don"
03.08.2022

Only Women Bleed

(Solo le Donne Sanguinano)

This is fact.
Men don't bleed.
They have no idea what a woman goes through.
They do not experience the rush of homones flowing throughout their body.
They do not have to experience the surge of emotions that distorts their emotions.
They do not have to put up with their mental state going chaotic.
How can they?
Because...
...only women bleed.

I know that men are from *Mars* & women are from *Venus*.
That's what I told you.
All you said to that was, *"That is so Pop"*.
Well that maybe true but what it doesn't negate its validity.
Men & women are different entities.
Men can never understand women.
We are from different planets.
There is no denying that.
Because...
...only women bleed.

Only women bleed!
Only women bleed!
Only women bleed!
Only women bleed!

"The Don"
03.08.2022

FIND WHAT WORKS FOR YOU
(Trova ciò che Funziona per Te)

You gotta find your *"groove"*.
You've gotta find your *"voice"*.
You've gotta find your *"mojo"*.
You've gotta find your *"muse"*.
You've just gotta find what works for you.

Don't try to *be someone else*.
Don't try to *copy others*.
Don't try to *imitate someone else*.
Don't *be someone you're not*.
You've just gotta find what works for you.

It could be *writing*.
It could be *painting*.
It could be *playing guitar*.
It could be *singing*.
Whatever it is…
…You've just gotta find what works for you.

"The Don"
04.08.2022

Mind Meld

(Fusione Mentale)

Your *thoughts* to my *thoughts*.
Your *ideas* to my *ideas*.
Your *feelings* to my *feelings*.
Your *mind* to my *mind*.
Mind meld.

We have become one.
I *see* what you see.
I *feel* what you feel.
I *think* what you think.
Mind meld.

You will never be the same again.
I will never be the same again.
We will never be the same again.
We have become one.
Mind meld.

One *entity*.
One *being*.
One *thought*.
One *consciousness*.
Mind meld.

"The Don"
04.08.2022

DO NOT LIVE IN FEAR

(Non Vivere nella PAURA)

Do not live in a *prison*.
Do not live in a *cage*.
Do not live in a *hole*.
Do not live in *isolation*.
Do not live in seclusion.
Do not live on *an island*.
DO NOT LIVE IN FEAR!

Do not be *scared*.
Do not be *alone*.
Do not be *by yourself*.
Do not be *worried*.
Do not be *terrified*.
Do not be *fearful*.
Do not be *isolated*.
DO NOT LIVE IN FEAR!

FEAR kills your *HE*♥*RT*.
FEAR kills your *mind*.
FEAR kills the *soul*.
FEAR kills the *spirit*.
FEAR kills *EVERYTHING!*
DO NOT LIVE IN FEAR!

"The Don"
05.08.2022

Apple of Knowledge

(Mela della Conoscenza)

Do not *take a bite*.
Do not *eat it*.
Do not *swallow it*.
Do not enjoy the *"Apple of Knowledge"*.

Ignorance is bliss.
Knowledge is dangerous.
So not bite it.
Do not eat it.
Do not taste the *"Apple of Knowledge"*.

Innocence is beautiful.
Knowledge is dangerous.
Unknown desires will be awoken.
Forbidden pleasures will be aroused.
Do not eat the *"Apple of Knowledge"*.

Whatever you do...
...do not eat the *"Apple of Knowledge"!*

"The Don"
08.08.2022

The Tree of LO♥E

(L'albero dell'AMORE)

We were walking along.
Not looking for anything in particular.
When we came upon this tree.
It was a *"Morton Bay Fig"* tree.
Indigenous to *"The Great Southern"* land.
The *"Land Down Under"*!
The land of *"Vegemite"*.
It was the *"Tree of LO♥E"*.

It had enormous roots coming out of its trunk.
Some were even hanging down from its branches.
And to our surprise, on the ground beneath its enormous branches, there was a huge HE♥RT.
It was made from red rose petals.
We were both amazed.
Who did this...?
...and why?
Then it came to me...
...it was the *"Universe"* speaking.
For we had stumbled across the *""Tree of LO♥E"*.

We *sat down inside it.*
We *lay down inside it.*
We *breathed in its beauty.*
We *felt its energy.*
We *understood its message.*
Under the *""Tree of LO♥E"*.

Not a word was spoken.
We *didn't say a word.*
We *didn't have to.*
We *didn't need too.*
We *understood its message.*
Then we got up & walked off.
Carrying its message with us.
Inside of us.
The message from the *"Tree of LO♥E"*.

"The Don"
08.08.2022

ECHO BEACH

(Spiaggia dell'Eco)

Echo Beach is far away in time.
Echo Beach is a *"State of mind"*.
Echo Beach is very hard to find.
Because...
...*Echo Beach* is in your mind.

How do I get there?
What do I have to do?
Is there a secret code?
Does it cost to enter?
Or...
...is it free?
Can you give me directions...?
...to get to *Echo Beach*?

Not everyone can find it.
It's not meant to be.
The path is difficult & treacherous.
It's hidden deep within the recesses of your mind.
You will have to travel long & far.
Make sure to take a packed lunch.
And plenty of water.
You need to stay hydrated.
Go with some friends...
...if you have any.
It's always more fun.
But when & if you get there.
If you are one of the lucky ones...
...to reach this fabled beach.
You won't be disappointed.

The problem is...
...you might never want to come back...
You might never want to return from...
...*Echo Beach*!

Echo Beach far away in time.
Echo Beach far away in time.
Echo Beach far away in time.
Echo Beach far away in time.

"The Don"
10.08.2022

Use Me as a "Bad" Example

(Usami Come un Male Esempio)

I failed my schooling.
I failed my parents.
I failed my university.
I failed my relationships.
I failed my parenting.
I failed my gender.
I failed my society.
I failed my religion.
I failed my morals.
I failed my ethics
I failed my principles.
I failed my integrity.
I failed my friends.
I failed my LO❤ERS.
I failed my LIFE.
So, why not use me as a *"bad"* example!

Actually, I'm a success story!

WTF!

"Who would've thought?"

(based on a conversation with Alex, my dope dealer)

"The Don"
11.08.2022

ONE OF "THEM"

(Uno di "loro")

One of the *abusers*.
One of the *oppressors*.
One of the *exploiters*.
You are on the floor.
You have closed the door.
You are no more.
Because you have become one of **"THEM"**!
That's if you do nothing.
Is that who you are?
Is that who you will become?
One of **"THEM"**!

Don't become one of **"THEM"**.
Become one of **"US"**.
Join the **"RESISTANCE"**.
The movement for change.

"The Don"
18.08.2022

Steamroller Blues

(Blues Rullo a Vapore)

I don't *wait for anyone.*
I don't *seek approval.*
I don't *stand still.*
I don't *hold back.*
'cause...
...*I'm a steamroller baby.*

I *always go forward.*
I *never take a backward step.*
I *will roll all over you.*
I *will not stop*
'cause...
...*I'm a steamroller baby.*

So, don't *get in my way.*
Don't *try & stop me.*
Don't *hang on to me.*
Don't *try & make me stay.*
'cause...
...*I'm a steamroller baby.*

I will not stop for *you.*
I will not stop for *anyone.*
I will not stop, *no matter what you say.*
I will not stop, I have only one way.
'cause...
...*I'm a steamroller baby.*

"I'm a steamroller baby
I'm 'bout to roll all over you
I'm a steamroller baby
I'm 'bout to roll all over you
I'm gonna inject your soul
With some sweet rock 'n' roll
And shoot you full of rhythm and blues."

Performed by: Elvis Presley
Songwriter: James Taylor

"The Don"
18.08.2022

Ignorance is Bliss

(L'ignoranza è Beatitudine)

It's better not to *look*.
It's better not to *question*.
It's better not to *search*.
It's better not to *seek*.
It's better not to *enquire*.
It's better not to *ask*.
Because...
...*ignorance is bliss.*

It's better to stay in the *dark*.
It's better to stay *uninformed*.
It's better to stay *delusional*.
It's better to stay in a *dream*.
It's better to stay *innocent*.
It's better to stay *ignorant*.
Because...
...*ignorance is bliss.*

Don't *look*.
Don't *question*.
Don't *search*.
Don't *seek*.
Don't *enquire*.
Don't *ask*.
Because...
...*you might not like what you find.*
That's why...
...*ignorance is bliss.*

Be blissful.
Stay ignorant.
Because...
...*ignorance is bliss.*

"The Don"
23.08.2022

Nothing Else Mattered

(Nient'altro Importava)

She *rejected it all*.
She *rejected everything*.
She *threw it all away*.
It meant nothing.
Our *friendship*.
Our *LO♥E*.
Our *connection*.
Our *energy*
Our *laughs*.
Our *talks*.
Our *ideas*.

They all meant nothing.
She threw them all away.
Because...
It seems that...
...*nothing else mattered.*

"The Don"
26.08.2022

NO MORE MR NICE GUY

(Niente Più Signor Bravo Ragazzo)

No more being *used*.
No more being told *"You're too easy!"*.
No more being the *"fool"*.
No more being *taken advantage of*.
No more being the *"third person "*.
No more being *fucked around*.
No more being the *"lacky"*.
No more being the *"go to guy"*.
No more being *manipulated*.
No more being the *"comedian"*.
No more being the *"joker"*.
No more being the *"idiot"*.
No more being *strung along*
No more being a *"puppet on a strung"*.
No more being *a "puppy dog"*.
No more being *made to grovel*.
No more being *made to beg*.
No more being *"taken for a ride"*.
No more being *the "last man standing"*.
No more being *taken for a "stooge"*.
No more being *your "gofer"*.
No more being *there for you when you are "down"*.
No more being *"Mr Reliable"*.
No more being *"Mr Nice Guy"*.

"The Don"
28.08 2022

You Are Too Needy

(Sei Troppo Bisognoso)

You give off a needy *smell*.
You have a needy *look*.
You *look* needy.
You *act* needy.
You *talk* needy.
You *walk* needy.
You *dress* needy.
You *eat* needy.
You *sleep* needy.
You *live* needy.
You are *too* needy.
Stop being so needy.
But...
...*EVERYONE* is needy.
It's just that...
...*SOME are more needy than OTHERS!*

"The Don"
28.08.2022

He is the One

(Lui è l'Uno)

He is the *one*.
He is the *one*.
He is the *one I'm looking for*.
He is the *one I want!*

He is the *one*.
He is the *one*.
He is the *one I'm looking for*.
He is the *one I want1*

He is the *one*.
He is the *one*.
He is the *one I'm looking for*.
He is the *one I want!*

He *ain't the one*.
He *ain't the one*.
He *ain't the one I'm looking for*.
He *ain't the one I want!*

He *ain't the one I'm looking for*.
He *ain't the one I want!*

He *ain't the one*.
He *ain't the one*.
He *ain't the one I'm looking for*.
He *ain't the one I want!*

He is the *one*.
He *ain't the one*.
He is the *one I'm looking for*.
He *ain't the one I want!*

"The Don"
30.08.2022

DO NOT THINK!

(Non pensare!)

This is a poem for non-thinkers.
Do not think.
Do not analyse.
Do not hypothesise.
Do not theorise.
Do not postulate.
Do not construct.
Do not deconstruct.
Do not suppose.
Do not juxtapose.
Do not fabricate.
Do not pontificate.
Do not subjugate.
Do not ruminate.
Do not deduce.
Do not induce.
Do not deduct.
Do not induct.
Do not infer.
Do not defer.
But most importantly...
...do NOT think!

STOP THINKING!

Thinking causes problems.
If you have to think...
...and I strongly advise you against that...
...think responsibly.
Also...
...I advise you to cap your thinking.
Put a limit on your thinking.
Say...
...only think for 10 minutes at a time...
...and then stop.
Whatever you do...
...do not OVER THINK!!!

Thinking is a disease.
Treat it as such!

Thinking is addictive.
Once you start you won't be able to stop.
It gets inside your blood.
It gets into your brain.
Pretty soon...
...you won't be able to sleep at night.
You'll lay awake for hours...
...*THINKING!*
You won't be able to turn it off.
You'll be FUCKED!
Thinking is insidious.
It's a CANCER!

So, I'll tell you again...
...do NOT THINK!!!

"The Don"
03.09.2022

Man Eater

(Mangiatrice di Uomini)

You're a *man eater*.
You're a *viper*.
You're a *black widow*.
You're a *vixen*.
You're an *enchantress*.
You're a *witch*.
You're a *voodoo child*.
You're a *wild child*.
You're a *Heathen child*
You're a *cosmic child*.
You're a *battler*.
You're a *fighter*.
You're an *Amazonian warrior*.
You're a *thrill seeker*.
You're an *adventurer*.
You're a *loner*.
You're a *hurricane*.
You're a *firestorm*.
You're an *enigma*.
You're a *narcissist*.
You're a man eater.

In fact, you don't discriminate...
...*you eat woman too!*

Can you eat me?

*"Watch out boy she'll chew you up.
She's a maneater."*

Songwriters: Daryl Hall/John Oates/Sara Allen

"The Don'
03.09.2022

Who is Happy Here?
(Chi è Felice Qui?)

No one wants to be here.
People are here because they have to be.
Due to circumstances.
Usually not of their own making.
Usually, they are stuck here.
They have to be here.
They do not have a choice.
They smile through clenched teeth.

Do they *want to be here?*
Do they *like to be here?*
Are they *happy here?*
Do they *want to stay here?*
Probably not.
Because...
...*who the fuck is happy here?*
Not me!
Are you?

Their *sorrows come down through the sky while they vegetate on their sofas.*
Their *dreams disappear when they wake up to go to work.*
Their *strains goes away when they come home and have to wash the dishes.*
Their *smiles are lost with the superficial connections that they even can't make.*
Nobody is happy here.

We go to *work.*
We go *home.*
We go to the *pub.*
We *see our friends on the weekend.*
We *hate our lives.*
We *hate our routine.*
In fact, we *hate ourselves.*
Because...
...*who is happy here?*
Not me!

It's *cold*.
It's *raining*.
My *head hurts*.
My *body screams*.
I'm *sad*.
It's *late*.
I *wake up*
It's all the same...
Nobody is happy.

We *have our dreams.*
We *live our lives.*
We *want a different life.*
We *seek a distant land.*
A land in which our HE❤RTS belong.
One day I will return to that place.
And then...
...*I will be happy.*
Because...
...*who is happy here?*

Miriam + "The Don"
04.09.2022

What's Between Your Legs?

(Cosa c'è tra le tue Gambe?)

NOTHING!

Why?

"The Don"
04.09.2022

I'm an Invitor

(Sono un Invitatore)

That's what I do.
I give them pathways.
I offer them opportunities.
A way out of their dismal lives.
They can take it or leave it.
It's up to them.
All I can do is invite them.
Because...
...*I'm an invitor.*

I invite souls to join together and indulge in good times.
I conjoin two individuals and open new roads.

I'm an invitor.
I want all the LO♥E to be spread.
I want everyone to enjoy the dance.
Always share with lonely souls.

I share the LO♥E.

"Miriam", "Little Stevie" & "The Don"
04.09.2022

The Midnight Rider

(Il Cavaliere di Mezzanotte)

Are you a *"Midnight Rambler"*?
Are you a *"Midnight Gambler"*?
Are you a *"Midnight Creeper"*?
Are you a *"Midnight Dealer"*?
Are you a *"Midnight Stealer"*?
Are you a *"Midnight Dreamer"*?
Are you a *"Midnight Schemer"*?
Are you a *"Midnight Talker"*?
Are you a *Midnight Caller?*
Are you a *"Midnight Walker"*?
Are you a *"Midnight Stalker"*?
Are you a *Midnight Streaker?*
Are you a *"Midnight Rager"*?
Are you a *"Midnight Faker"*?
Are you a *"Midnight Staller"*?
Are you a *"Midnight Baller"*?
Are you a *"Midnight Rider"*?

"The Don"
08.09.2022

THE CHALLENGE

(La Sfida)

That's the *point of the game*.
That's what *thrills you*.
That's what *excites you!*
That's what *turns you on*.
That's what *drives you*.

The *pursuit*.
The *conquering*.
The *consuming*.
The *devouring*.
The *slaughter*.
The *conquest*.
The *vanquishing*.
The *moving on*.

The challenge has been met.
The challenge has been defeated.
The challenge has been conquered.

Now to the next...
...*challenge!*

"The Don"
09.09.2022

Unhinged

(*Scatenato*)

Are you *completely crazy?*
Are you *stark raving mad?*
Are you a *complete looney bin?*
Are you *insane?*
Are you *mental?*
Are you a *psycho?*
Are you *outta of your head?*
Are you *completely outta of your fucking mind?*
Are you *completely fucking unhinged?*

Have you *lost your way?*
Have you *lost your direction?*
Have you *forgotten where you wanna go?*
Have you *lost your sense of purpose?*
Have you *lost your frivolity?*
Have you *lost your gaiety?*
Have you *lost your humour?*
Have you *lost your laughter?*
Have you *lost your FUN?*
Have you *lost your dignity?*
Have you *lost your self-respect?*
Have you *forgotten who you are?*
Have you *forgotten who you wanna be?*
Have you *lost yourself?*
Are you *completely fucking unhinged?*

Don't worry!
You're not alone!
Because...
...I am too!

"The Don"
15.09.2022

Tattooed Woman

(Donna Tatuata)

This a fantasy poem.

I love a *Tattooed Woman*.
I love to talk to a *Tattooed Woman*.
I love to listen to a *Tattooed Woman*.
I love to smoke with a *Tattooed Woman*.
I love to drink with a *Tattooed Woman*.
I love to get STONED with a *Tattooed Woman*.
I love to get HIGH with a *Tattooed Woman*.
I love to hold a *Tattooed Woman*.
I love to kiss a *Tattooed Woman*.
I love to kiss the tattoos of a *Tattooed Woman*.
I love to undress a *Tattooed Woman*.
I LO♥E to make LO♥E to a *Tattooed Woman*.
I love a *Tattooed Woman*.

"The Don"
16.09.2022

(Punk)

Are you a *"Punk"*?
So, you wanna be a *"Punk"*?
Do you wanna be *naughty*?
Do you wanna be *rebellious*?
Do you want to be *different*?
Why not be a "Punk"?

There's a bit of *"Johnny Rotten"* in all of us.
How about a bit of *"Sid Vicious"* attitude?
Or what about *"The Slits'"* rebelliousness?
Maybe some *"Patti Smith"*, the mother of *"Punk Poets"*?
You can be a *"Punk"* too!

It's not what you *wear*.
It's not what you *look like*.
It's not what job you *have*.
Or what *education or school you went to*.
No...
...it's about *"Tude"*...
...*ATTITUDE!*
A *"Punk"* attitude!
Be a *"Punk"*!

"The Don"
23.09.2022

I'm Not Going to Participate

(Non ho Intenzione di Partecipare)

I'm not going to *get involved*.
I'm not going to *speak*.
I'm not going to *argue*.
I'm not going to *respond*.
Because...
...I'm not going to participate.

I'm not going to *pontificate*.
I'm not going to *adjudicate*.
I'm not going to *subjugate*.
I'm not going to *discriminate*.
Because...
...I'm not going to participate.

I'll be *silent*.
I'll be *quiet*.
I'll be *numb*.
I'll be *dumb*.
Because...
...I'm not going to participate.

I'll hold my *tongue*.
I'll bite my *lips*.
I'll shut my *eyes*.
I'll close my *ears*.
Because...
...I'm not going to participate.

I will not *respond*.
I will not *participate in*...
...*stupidity!*

"The Don"
23.09.2022

Falls in Love with Wealth

(Si Innamora della Ricchezza)

What a *mistake*.
What an *error of judgement*.
What a *gamble*.
What an *idiot*.
He should have fallen in LO♥E with humans.

Not *money*.
Not *prestige*.
Not *security*.
Not *privilege*.
Not with *comfort*.
He should NOT have fallen in LO♥E with wealth.

"The Don"
23.09.2020

I Disagree with Everything You've Said So Far!

(Non sono d'accordo con tutto quello che hai detto finora!)

Shock me!!!!!
Do I have to explain how the *"System"* works?
We live in a *"Capitalist"* system.
This is one which puts money before people.
Everything is focused on making money.
Its only goal is to make profit.
And lots of it.
At the expense of everything else.
Even human life.
We are *expendable to making profit*.
We are *not worth much*.
We are *quite cheap*.
And *very disposable*.
We're *just a commodity...*
...to be bought & sold.

Do you understand now?
NO?
That's a shame.
Not for me...
...but for you!

I have already said too much.
I have nothing else to say.
Except...
...surprise me!
Tell me something I've not heard before!
Because...
...I've heard it ALL before!
And...
...it's all SHIT!

"The Don"
24.09.2022

My Demons

(I Miei Demoni)

At night...
...they *come out to play*.
They like to *have a good time*.
They like to *cause mischief*...
...*with me!*
They like to *play with me*.
They like to *fuck me around*.
They like to *torment me*.
They like to *provoke me*.
They like to *incite me*.
They like to *destroy me*.
They like to *dance on my grave*.

My demons...
...*know all the tricks*.
They know *all about me*.
They know *everything about me*
They know all the *right buttons to push*.
They know how to get *under my skin*.
They know how to get *into my head*.
They know how to *break my HE♥RT*.
They know how to *destroy me*.
Because...
...*my demons are inside of me!*

"The Don"
28.09.2022

With Age Comes Experience!
(Con l'età Arriva l'Esperienza!)

Don't let age *fool* you
Don't let age *inhibit* you.
Don't let age *stop* you.
Don't let age *"pigeon-hole"* you.
Don't let age *define* you.
Don't let age *control* you.
Because...
...*with age comes experience!*

Age is a *number*.
Age is a *concept*.
Age is a *"human construct"*.
Age is a *myth*.
Age is an *illusion*.
Age is *physical*.
Age is *subjective*.
So, remember...
...*with age comes experience!*

Don't let my age fool you...
...I might be old...
...but I have *experience!*

Because...
...*with age comes experience!*

"Do you have experience?"
"Are you experienced?"

"The Don"
29.09.2022

The Head/He♥rt Dichotomy

(La Dicotomia Testa/Cuore)

When the head says one thing...
...and the HE♥RT wants something else.

"The Don"
29.09.2022

Divine Intervention

(Intervento Divino)

I'm seeking *celestial intervention.*
Because...
... I need something.
So, it might as well be *Divine.*
Cosmic will do just as well.
It doesn't matter to me.
Because...
... I need something.
I need some *intervention…*
…*Divine intervention!*

"The Don"
01.10.2022

Hey, Hey Ho

(Ehi, Ehi Ho)

Hey, hey ho...
...let's go.
Let's *get started.*
Let's *take this beauty on the road.*
Let's *take her for a ride.*
Let's *see what she can do.*
Let's *put the foot on the pedal.*

Let's *show her the sky.*
The beautiful land.
The amazing places.
She wants to go.

And we sing...
...hey, hey ho!
Hey, hey ho!

Put your *shit out.*
Exchange your *energy.*
Let's go to the *beach.*
Let's go to the *sun.*
Let's *come back to the sky.*

Let's *live life like there's no tomorrow.*
Let's *see things without using our eyes*
Let's *feel like we've never felt before.*
Let's *burn & not fade away!*

Singing...
...hey, hey ho!
Hey, hey ho!

Hey, hey ho!
Hey, hey ho!

Miriam + "The Don"
01.10.2022

Where Have They All Gone?

(Dove Sono Finiti Tutti?)

Where have all the flowers gone?
They were here a long time ago.
Where have all the plants gone?
They were here a long time ago.
Where have all the animals gone?
They were here a long time ago.
Where has all the wildlife gone?
They were here a long time ago.
Where has all the happiness gone?
It was here a long time ago.
Where have all the ideals gone?
They were here a long time ago.
Where has all the humanity gone?
It was here a long time ago.
Where has all the spirituality gone?
It was here a long time ago.
Where have all the people gone?
They were here a long time ago.
Where have all the gone?

They were here a long time ago.
They were here a long time ago.
Here a long time ago.

"The Don"
05.10.2022

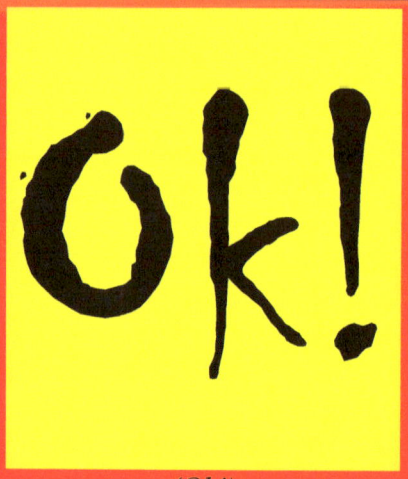

(Ok!)

I *got it!*
I *understand!*
It's *clear to me now!*
I *see the picture!*
I *know the score.*
I *get what it's all about!*
I *know what's going down!*
It's *cool!*
I'm *nobody's fool!*
I'm *a realist too!*
So...
...I got it!
It's ok!

"The Don"
05.10.2022

False Hopes

(False Speranze)

"Abandon all hope ye who enter here"
That's what *Dante Alighieri* stated at the beginning of his journey into the *"Inferno"* from his masterpiece *"The Divine Comedy"*.
When you travel on your journey from *Hell, Purgatory & finally Heaven*.
Hell is Earth...
...our life of turmoil & struggle.
Of...
...pain & suffering.
...loss & guilt.
...torment & delusion
Through to, hopefully...
...reconciliation & redemption.
And eventually, maybe, if you're lucky, to...
...Nirvana.
...enlightenment.
..."The Light".

But do not *have expectations*.
Do not *harbour desires*.
Do not *seek illusions*.
Do not *carry hopes*.
Because for certain they will be *"false hopes"*.
They will *weigh you down*.
They will be an *albatross around your neck*.
They will be a *weight upon your shoulders*.
They will be a *cross you will have to carry on your back*.
They will be *worms inside your brain*.
You will *definitely fall & stumble*.
They will *blind you*.
They will *fill your mind & HE♥RT with delusions*.
And ultimately, you will *fail*.

So, I say to you...
..."Leave all false hopes behind & travel to the light".

In fact, most hopes are false!

"The Don"
07.10.202

The Withdrawal Method
(Il Metodo di Ritiro)

It's when you *pull out*.
It's when you *exit a situation*.
It is when *you leave...*
...a place you a no longer wanted in.
A place you are no *longer desired in*.
A place where you no *longer belong*.
A place you no *longer want to be in*.
A situation you no *longer need...*
...or no longer needs you.
This is when you use *"The Withdrawal Method"*.

Just pack your bags & leave.
Do not pack too much.
It's best to travel light.
Exit *"stage left"*.
Don't make a *"song & dance"*.
Just leave quietly...
...without saying a word.
No need for long *"goodbyes"*.
Or *"pithy"* speeches.
Or memorable *"last words"*.
"The Withdrawal Method" does it all for you.
It has your *"back"*.

All you have to do is walk away.
But make sure to...
...NOT turn BACK!

"The Don"
07.10.2022

I DON'T FIND YOU SEXUALLY ATTRACTIVE

(Non ti Trovo Sessualmente Attraente)

"I don't find you sexually attractive!"
That's what she said.
WTF!
Those words hit me like a machine gun.
I wasn't ready for them.
I was in shock.
I was traumatised.
I started to cry.
I packed my bag...
...said goodbye & walked out.
She said, *"do you want to take the bottle of wine?"*
"No! You keep it!", I replied.
And I left.
She closed her door behind me.
I never looked back!

"The Don"
08.10.2022

I Cannot Piss Straight

(Non Posso Pisciare Dritto)

I was standing in front of the bowel.
I started to piss...
...staring straight ahead.
...as one should.
...staring at my reflection in the mirror.
...I looked pretty good for my age I thought to myself.
...with a slight grin on my face.
...and a raised eyebrow.
When...
...I felt something warm & fuzz.
...not inside me though.
...rather down my right leg.
Oh SHIT!
I thought to myself...
...don't tell me...
...it's my piss?
Oh FUCK!
NO!
It FUCKING is!
I look of horror & disgust covered my face & body.
SHIT!
"I'm pissing myself!"
"FUCK I HATE THAT!"

Sometimes, I forget to sit down on the bowl.
Because that's the only way to make sure that the piss goes where it's supposed to go...
...into the FUCKING bowl.

I have experienced some strange directions my piss would take...
...before I acquiesced, surrendered & accepted my fate...
...that I was condemned to piss sitting down!
"This is what I've been reduced to!", I thought.
One time I remember clearly, I pissed in 3 directions simultaneously...
1 directly straight ahead & 2 on either side...
...none of them actually going where they were supposed to go...
...in the FUCKING bowl!

"The Don"
08.10.2022

She Uses Sex as Therapy
(Lei Usa il Sesso Come Terapia)

That explains everything.
Now I understand her.
I understand her actions.
I was also used as therapy
And that's alright.
That's ok!
I understand.
She's found something that works for her.
Maybe...
...for a short time.
...at least.
Until the next hit.
We all need therapy.
Some more than others.
And more often than not sex is our therapy.
She used sex as therapy.
And it's not a bad therapy to have!

"The Don"
10.10.2022

My Soil is Fertile

(Il mio Terreno è Fertile)

Plant yourself on me.
Set *your roots in me.*
Find *stability in me.*
Feel *secure in me.*
Feel *protected in me.*
Feel *sheltered in me.*
Feel *comforted in me.*
Feel *cared for in me.*
Feel *LO*❤*E in me.*
Grow in me.
Blossom in me.
Bloom in me.
Fruit in me.
Sleep in me.

"The Don"
11.10.2022

𝕴 𝕰𝖝𝖎𝖘𝖙!

(Io Esisto!)

I am NOT *invisible*.
I am NOT a *ghost*.
I am NOT a *"non-person"*
I am NOT a *"non-entity"*
I am NOT a *"nothing"*.
I am NOT a *"has-been"*.
I am NOT a *"vague thought."*
I am NOT an *"after thought"*.
I EXIST!

I BREATHE.
I SEE.
I HEAR.
I TOUCH.
I FEEL.
I THINK.
I have FEELINGS.
I LIVE.
I EXIST!

I EXIST!

I EXIST!

I EXIST!

Do you?
Or so you think!
Of course you do!

"The Don"
12.10.2022

REBOOT

(Riavviare)

Sometimes that's what you have to do.
There is no alternative.
You have to shut the system down...
...completely!
There is no other way.
There is nothing else you can do.
A complete *"reset"* is required.
That's the only way...
...the only way to start anew.
Start a fresh.
Start again...
...from the beginning.
Start a new game.
Maybe you'll do better this time.
You MUST reboot!

There are no guarantees that it will come back on.
There's no certainty that it will reboot.
It might be unsuccessful.
That's the risk you take
But there's nothing else you could've done.
Once in the *"reboot"* phase...
...there nothing you can do.
It may never come out!
But, there's no other way.
There is no alternative.

"Good luck...!"
"...in your wait."

"Do you feel lucky?"

"The Don"
12.10.10.2022

I Am a Player

(Sono un Giocatore)

She said, *"I am a player!"*.
Yes, that's what she said.

What is a *"player"*?

A person who is single and is out to date anybody he or she wants. It is as simple as that!
A person who has many lovers.
Juggling a series of relatively brief and sometimes over-lapping intimate relationships.
Seeing multiple people (with or without you knowing about it) that doesn't have consideration towards your feelings, and will tell you anything it takes to *"play"* you into bed.
They're not looking for commitment, but will *"play"* games to make you think they are.
"A player" doesn't treat humans like a human.
Rather they treat them like sexual objects.
The term usually refers to a man.

What does it mean when a girl is a *"player"*?
It usually means one of three things...
...none of them good!
One, she is cheating on somebody with you.
Two, she is embarrassed by you.
Or three, she is *"playing"* you.

Is it *"bad"* to be a *"player"*?
It's someone who will most likely cheat on you.
It's someone who's not that trustworthy and who may say things just to get you into bed or just to get some action. In other words, yeah being a" player" is generally considered bad for most girls.

"Have you ever been called a "player"?"
"Are you a "player"?"

"The Don"
13.10.2022

Have a Good LIFE!

(Hanno una Buona vita!)

My father died in the early hours of the 25th May 2008.
At RPA (Royal Prince Alfred) Hospital in Camperdown,
After a short illness.
He was eighty-three years old.
He had contracted "septicaemia (sepsis)".
And it had spread throughout his body,
Resulting in massive organ failure.
There was nothing the doctors could do.
Except pump him with antibiotics.
Which prolonged his life for an extra three weeks.

Watching him die in those last weeks,
I learnt that it's better to come to terms with your demons...
...put them to rest,
...earlier in your life,
...when you can!
...when you have the strength,
...and courage to confront them.
Rather than...
...wait and fight with them,
...when you're dying!

My father was fighting his demons right till the end!

It was NOT a good death!

So, the moral of this story...
...the moral of this poem is:

Make sure to have a good LIFE...
...so that you can have a good DEATH!

"The Don"
15.10.2022

Who Are You Fucking Today?

(Chi Stai Scopando Oggi?)

"It's none of your FUCKING business!"

"The Don"
17.10.2022

It's Just Life

(È Solo la Vita)

It's just life...
...that's all!
Just life...
...that's it!.
It's just LIFE!

"The Don"
21.10.2022

Finally, I'm a Hippie

(Finalmente Sono un Hippie)

I've *"made it!"*
"I'm a Hippie!"

I'm burning *"Patchouli"* incense.
Finally, I'm a "Hippie"!

"The Don"
20.10.2022

I DON'T NEED MORE INFORMATION

(Non Ho Bisogno di Ulteriori Informazioni)

I don't need more information...
...to feed my imagination!

"The Don"
21.10.2022

Books written by "The Don"

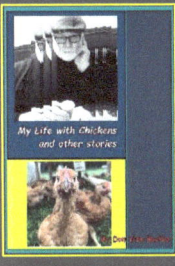
"My Life with Chickens & other stories: I Pity the Poor Immigrant"
Published:
10th September, 2019
Autobiography Book 1:
0 – 12 years old

"Poems for Misfits, Miscreants, Misanthropes, Mavericks, Losers & Malcontents!"
Published:
10th June, 2020
Book of Poems 1

"Poems for Troubled Minds & Trouble Hearts"
Published:
10th August, 2020

Book of Poems 2

"My Life in a CULT & other stories: Everybody Must Get STONED!"
Published:
10th September, 2020
Autobiography Book 2:
15 – 30 years old

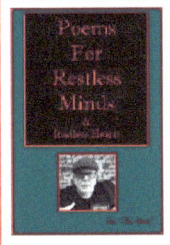
"Poems for Restless Minds & Restless Hearts"
Published:
10th October, 2020
Book of Poems 3

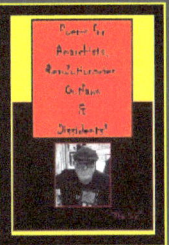
"Poems for Anarchists, Revolutionaries, Outlaws & Dissidents!"
Published:
10th November, 2020

Book of Poems 4

"Poems for Non-Thinkers & Eccentrics"
Published:
10th December, 2020
Book of Poems 5

"The Rantings of a Madman"
Published:
10th January, 2021

Book of Poems 6

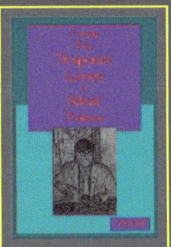
"Poems for Desperate Lovers & Silent Voices"
Published:
10th February, 2021
Book of Poems 7

"Poems for Tormented Minds & Tortured Souls"
Published:
10th March, 2021
Book of Poems 8

All available ONLY online

Books written by "The Don"

"Poems for ALIENS, Outsiders, Outcasts & other STRANGE BEINGS!"
Published: 10th April, 2021
Book of Poems 9

"Poems for Beings From Another Planet"
Published: 10th May, 2021
Book of Poems 10

"Poems for Mindless Beings & Lost Souls"
Published: 10th June, 2021
Book of Poems 11

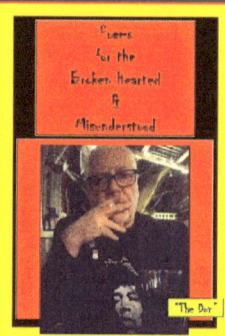

"Poems for the Broken Hearted & Misunderstood
Published: 10th July, 2021
Book of Poems 12

"Poems for Poems for the Bewildered, Dazed & Confused"
10th August, 2021
Book of Poems 13

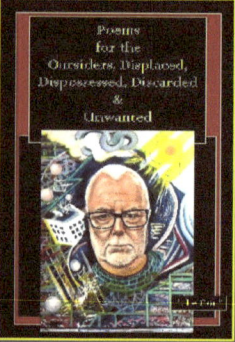

"Poems for the Outsiders, Displaced, Dispossessed, Discarded & Unwanted"
Published: 10th Sept, 2021
Book of Poems 14

All available ONLY online

"Poems for Secret Agents, Phantom Agents, Agents of Change, Agent Provocateurs & Agents of Chaos"
Published: 10th Oct, 2021
Book of Poems 15

"Poems for Disenchanted, Disillusioned & Delusional"
Published: 10th November, 2021
Book of Poems 16

Books written by "The Don"

"Poems for the Stoners, drugos, ACID takers & Psychedelic LO♥ERS (Everybody Must Get Stoned)"
Published: 10th December, 2021
Book of Poems 17

"Poems for Anarchists, Rebels & Revolutionaries
Published: 10th January, 2022
Book of Poems 18

"Poems for Rebels, Radicals & Revolutionaries (Viva la Révolution!)"
Published: 10th February, 2022
Book of Poems 19

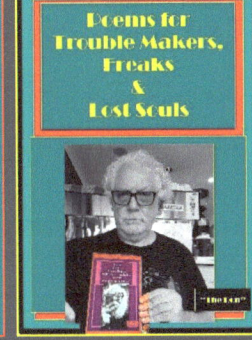

"Poems for Trouble Makers, Freaks & Lost Souls"
Published: 10th March 2022
Book of Poems 20

"Poems for Zombies & the Walking Dead"
Published: 10th April 2022
Book of Poems 21

"Poems for Non-Conformists (Never conform!)"
Published: 10th May 2022
Book of Poems 22

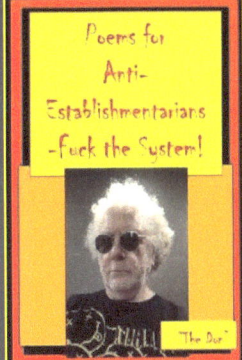

"Poems for Anti-Establishment-arians -Fuck the System!"
Published: 10th June 2022
Book of Poems 23

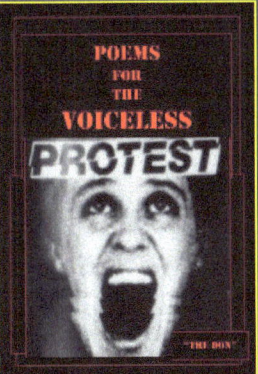

"Poems for the Voiceless"
Published: 10th July 2022
Book of Poems 24

All available ONLY online

Books written by "The Don"

"Poems for the Fearless"

Published:
10th August 2022

Book of Poems 25

"Poems for the PEACEMAKERS: Make peace NOT war!"

Published:
10th March 2023

Book of Poems 26

All available ONLY

www.ingramcontent.com/pod-product-compliance
Lightning Source LLC
Chambersburg PA
CBHW041502010526
44107CB00049B/1630